Once upon a time, billions of years ago, there was ... nothing!
Yep, that's right, nothing at all.
No light, no heat, no stars, no planets, no peanut butter, just, well ... nothing.

Or at least, nothing very much — only an infinitesimally small, but incredibly hot, dot of something that suddenly ...

... EXPLODED!

Scientists call this explosion the BIG BANG, and they think it was the beginning of everything — the beginning of the UNIVERSE.✷

✷ Some scientists think that before our Universe came along, there must have been an earlier one that started to shrink. And it went on shrinking until absolutely everything in it was squashed together into a tiny spot, smaller than the smallest seed.

A CARTOON HISTORY OF THE EARTH

Volume 1: The Birth of the Earth

Written by
Jacqui Bailey

Illustrated by
Matthew Lilly

Kids Can Press

For Cleo — who's definitely a star
J. B.
For Jack and Thomas
M. L.

With thanks to Carole Stott
for her expert help in getting
the facts right, and
to Martin Jenkins for
straightening us out on the
bacteria front.

Copyright © Two's Company 2001

Published by permission of A&C Black
(Publishers) Limited, London

Published in Canada by   Published in the U.S. by
Kids Can Press Ltd.   Kids Can Press Ltd.
29 Birch Avenue   2250 Military Road
Toronto, ON M4V 1E2   Tonawanda, NY 14150

www.kidscanpress.com

Printed in Hong Kong by
Wing King Tong Company Limited

The hardcover edition of this book
is smyth sewn casebound.

The paperback edition of this book is
limp sewn with a drawn-on cover.

CM 01 0 9 8 7 6 5 4 3 2 1
CM PA 01 0 9 8 7 6 5 4 3 2 1

Canadian Cataloguing in Publication Data

Bailey, Jacqui
The birth of the earth
(The cartoon history of the earth ; 1)
Includes index.

ISBN 1-55337-071-6 (bound)
ISBN 1-55337-080-5 (pbk.)

1. Big bang theory – Comic books, strips,
etc. – Juvenile literature. I. Lilly, Matthew.
II. Title. III. Series: Bailey, Jacquie.
Cartoon history of the earth ; 1.

QB991.B54B34 2001   j523.1'8
C00-933319-3

Kids Can Press is a Nelvana company

As you read this book, you'll see some words in capital letters — **LIKE THIS**. These words are listed in the Glossary on pages 30–31, where there is more information about them. And when you see the asterisk (✹), look for a box on the page that also has an asterisk. This box gives you even more information on the topic.

The Big Bang happened about 13 billion years ago, and it was the most powerful explosion there has ever been — greater than all the world's bombs put together.

But although it was enormously bright and enormously hot, the Big Bang wasn't very *noisy*! In fact, you wouldn't have heard anything at all. ✳

✳ Sound travels in waves, but waves need something to move through, such as air or water. Nothing existed before the Big Bang, so there wasn't anything to carry the sound waves when the Big Bang went off.

Just seconds after the Big Bang, a tiny, seething mass of energy appeared — a baby Universe.

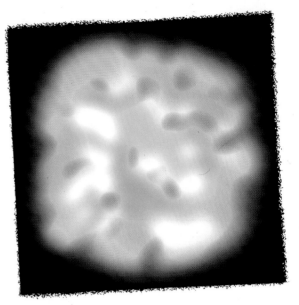

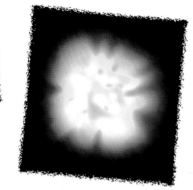

Baby it might have been, but it was still indescribably hot, and it was getting *bigger* and spreading outward all the time.

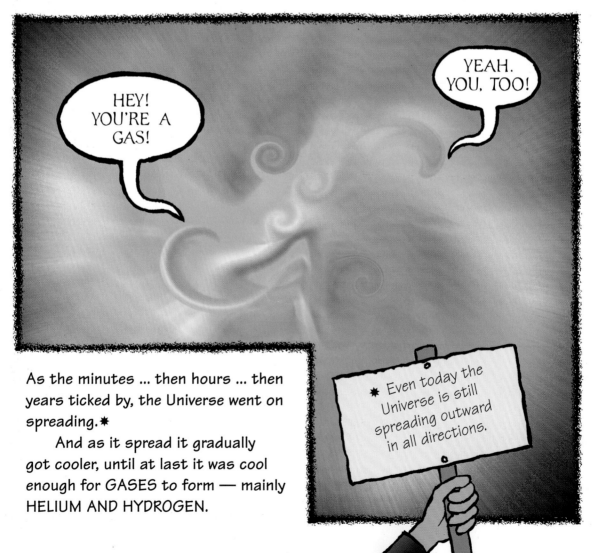

HEY! YOU'RE A GAS!

YEAH. YOU, TOO!

As the minutes ... then hours ... then years ticked by, the Universe went on spreading.✷

And as it spread it gradually got cooler, until at last it was cool enough for GASES to form — mainly HELIUM AND HYDROGEN.

✷ Even today the Universe is still spreading outward in all directions.

But the gases weren't spread evenly through the young Universe. And about 300 000 years after the Big Bang, some of them began clumping together into clouds.

URRGH! I'M FEELING DIZZY.

Not the fluffy, cuddly sort of clouds we see on Earth, mind you. These were huge, whirling clouds. They were the beginnings of GALAXIES.

As each growing galaxy whirled, ✳ it pulled in more and more gas and got lumpier and lumpier, until ... something amazing happened.

✳ There are thousands of millions of galaxies whirling around in the Universe. They come in all shapes and sizes: spiral ones, egg-shaped ones and bulgy, blobby, no-shape-at-all ones.

A STAR WAS BORN!

Well, zillions of stars actually. Crowds and *crowds* of stars, like gigantic swarms of fireflies.

ME, THREE.

I'M A STAR.

ME, TOO.

Once they'd started, the galaxies *went on* giving birth to stars, too. In fact, new stars are being born all the time. But no star shines forever ...

GREAT BALLS OF FIRE!

Stars are just giant balls of blazingly hot gases — mostly hydrogen and helium.
  They are *so* fantastically hot that deep in the center of a star the hydrogen gas is changed — into more helium. Then, when the hydrogen in the center is all used up, the helium changes, too, into other stuff like carbon or iron. ✳

✳ A more scientific way of describing all the stuff that makes up a star is to call it **MATTER.** Everything in the Universe is made up of some type of matter (including you, me and the garden fence), whether it's a solid, a liquid or a gas.

Although stars live for millions and millions of years, eventually they run out of helium as well, and then they die.

Most stars dwindle away into a cold, black, burnt-out thing that looks like it was left too long on a barbecue.

But sometimes a star will *blow up* —
in a spectacular explosion known as a SUPERNOVA.

When this happens, much of the material that made up the star is hurled out into space. And then ... guess what?

WOOOOSH!

It mixes with the other gases that hang around in space, forms more gas clouds and makes *new stars*.

YOO-HOO! HERE I AM!

So where does the Earth fit in to all this? Well, about eight billion years or so after the Big Bang, a new star formed near the edge of a swirling spiral galaxy.
It was our SUN.

Now our Sun isn't all that unusual, as stars go. There are bigger and brighter stars. Ours is just medium sized and medium bright.

But after it formed, there was a cloudy *disc* of leftover gas and DUST still whirling around it.

And that's when something unusual did happen. The tiny specks of dust in the disc started bumping and thumping into each other. And as they did so, some of them stuck together to make *lumps.*

Then the lumps began smashing and bashing into each other, and they grew into bigger lumps.

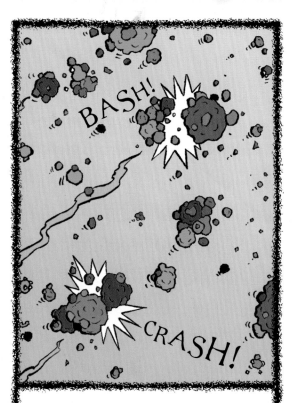

And the bigger lumps bashed into each other and became *really big* lumps ... and then the biggest lumps of all began to pull gases toward them. ✱

SPLAT!

✱ The dust and the gas were pulled together by something called **GRAVITY**. Gravity is a force that pulls one thing toward another. Everything in the Universe has gravity. Bigger objects with more matter in them have stronger gravity than smaller ones. Although the further away you are from an object, the less its gravity pulls on you.

PHEW! PEACE AT LAST.

Millions of years later, when everything finally settled down, the disc of gas and dust had gone. In its place were nine *huge* lumps (and lots and lots of smaller ones) all zooming around the Sun.

The huge lumps, of course, are the PLANETS. Some of the smaller ones ended up as ASTEROIDS. Others are MOONS and COMETS — but we'll talk about those in a moment. The point is, together with the Sun, they make up what we call our SOLAR SYSTEM.✱

HI THERE!

4

6

5

2

1

3

✱ In the 1990s, astronomers began to search our galaxy for other stars that had planets going around them. And they discovered some that did! Now we know for sure that our Solar System isn't the only one in the galaxy, even though the others are much too far away for us to see — yet.

7

9

Once they sorted themselves out, the planets became very well behaved — and they've stayed that way ever since.

11

10

8

The Solar System
1 Sun
2 Mercury
3 Venus
4 Earth
5 Mars
6 Asteroid belt
7 Jupiter
8 Saturn
9 Uranus
10 Neptune
11 Pluto

Each planet swings around and around the Sun along its own path or ORBIT. They all travel in the same direction, and they all keep their distance from each other. (Except for Pluto, that is — which every now and then elbows in front of Neptune!) And the third planet from the Sun is ours — good old Earth!

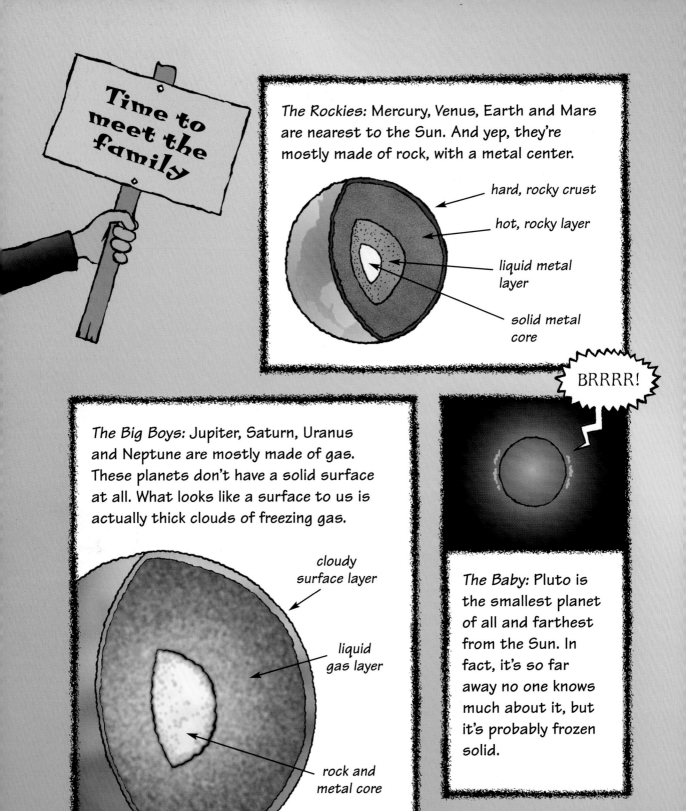

Time to meet the family

The Rockies: Mercury, Venus, Earth and Mars are nearest to the Sun. And yep, they're mostly made of rock, with a metal center.

- hard, rocky crust
- hot, rocky layer
- liquid metal layer
- solid metal core

BRRRR!

The Big Boys: Jupiter, Saturn, Uranus and Neptune are mostly made of gas. These planets don't have a solid surface at all. What looks like a surface to us is actually thick clouds of freezing gas.

- cloudy surface layer
- liquid gas layer
- rock and metal core

The Baby: Pluto is the smallest planet of all and farthest from the Sun. In fact, it's so far away no one knows much about it, but it's probably frozen solid.

Below the clouds, the gas is squashed so tightly together it becomes liquid. And at the center there's a lump of boiling hot rock and metal. All four gas planets have thin rings made of chunks of rocky ice spinning around them.

Moons: Moons are smaller lumps of rock or rock and ice that orbit the planets.

Not all of the planets have moons. Mercury and Venus don't have any, Earth has one, and Mars has two. But the giant gas planets have lots.

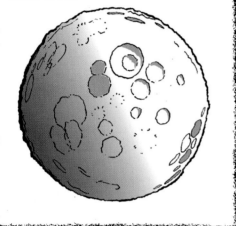

Asteroids: These are lumps of rock that orbit the Sun. Some are the size of a small moon, others are no bigger than a mountain. Millions of them travel in a band called the asteroid belt that lies between Mars and Jupiter.

It's possible that the asteroid belt is all that's left of a small, rocky planet that tried to form, but then broke up again.

Comets: Comets are like big, dirty snowballs. Mostly, they hang about on the edges of the Solar System, way beyond Pluto. But a few of them follow huge, looping orbits that bring them closer to the Sun for a time.

WHEEEEEEE!

When this happens, the comet starts to sizzle in the Sun's heat and gives off gas and dust that stream out behind it. And when it gets close enough, it shines in the light of the Sun so that for a while it looks like a giant firework zipping through the Solar System.

Anyway, to get back to our story ...

All that crashing and banging really heated things up. At first the Earth was so hot it was like a big, bubbling ball of boiling toffee. It slowly cooled down, though,✳ and as it did a crinkly, crusty surface formed around the outside.

I'M HOT, HOT, HOT!

✳ Boy, was it slow! We're talking millions of years, here! In fact, scientists think the Earth formed about 4600 million years ago and then it took about 600 million years to cool down enough to form a crust.

Not that the surface was all that solid, mind you. Not at first, anyway. In the beginning, it was continually being heaved up and ripped apart by volcanoes and earthquakes.

BOOM!

And all the time this was going on, it was also belching out clouds of ash and hot liquid rock, and giving out lots of smelly gases!

PHEW! WHAT A STINK!

The gases didn't go away, either. Instead of floating off into space, Earth's gravity held on to them.

Eventually there was a layer of gases all around the planet. We had an ATMOSPHERE.

Not any kind of atmosphere you could breathe, of course. These gases were mostly *poisonous*. But along with the poisonous gases, like methane and carbon dioxide, there was also water vapor. ✱

✱ We usually think of water as a liquid. But when water is heated by even a small amount, it becomes a gas called water vapor. At first, the Earth was so hot that all of its water existed as gas.

Now, where you have an atmosphere, you have ... *weather!* And lousy weather it was, too. Nothing but storms, thunder and lightning.

cRRA AACK!

Up in the atmosphere, the water vapor cooled down, became liquid and fell ... as rain.

It rained ... and it rained ... and it rained! And then it rained some more.

And the rain made puddles,

then ponds,

then lakes,

and finally it made oceans ...
And that's when things got really exciting!

What's so exciting about water?

Well, if we didn't have water, none of us would be here, that's what! In fact, most scientists think that it isn't possible for *any life* to exist without liquid water. At least, not any kind of life we can imagine. Every living thing on Earth needs water to survive, whether it's a tree, an elephant or a bug.

WATER!

LOOKS PRETTY. THINK ANYTHING LIVES THERE?

And guess what? Earth is the *only planet* in our Solar System that has liquid water. And, as far as we know, it's the *only place* in the Solar System that has any *life*!

So how come we have liquid water and the other planets don't? Well, it's all about being in the right place. The Earth is just the right *distance* from the Sun.

Any closer and our water would boil away in the Sun's heat.

Any further away and it would freeze.

But that's not all. The atmosphere helps, too. On the side of the Earth that faces *toward* the Sun, the atmosphere works like a giant sunshade. It *blocks out some of the Sun's* ferocious heat so we don't get too warm.

Sun's rays

✽ As the planets travel around the Sun, they are also spinning like tops. The Earth takes 365 ¼ days (one year) to travel once around the Sun, and it takes 23 hours and 56 minutes (one day) to turn itself around once.
As the Earth spins, different parts of it face toward the Sun's light and then turn away again. When parts of the Earth face toward the Sun, we say they're in daytime, and when they face away from the Sun, we say they're in nighttime.

And on the side of the Earth that faces away from the Sun, the atmosphere works like a giant blanket. This time it *holds in some of the heat so we don't get too cold.* ✽

Okay, that's enough about water. Let's get back to our oceans ... because, of course, water wasn't the only thing in them.

As the rain fell, it washed other CHEMICALS from the atmosphere down with it, and all these chemicals sloshed around in the oceans like enormous bowls of rather strange soup.

And this is where the magic comes in. Because although we're pretty sure *what* happened next, no one really knows *how* it happened!

SHAZZAM!

✳ There are lots of different ideas and beliefs about how life began on Earth. Many scientists think the chemicals changed because they got zapped by lightning — yep, the storms were still going on!

In any event, what did happen was that some of the chemicals in the soup changed. They turned into incredibly small and very simple little blobs of *living stuff* called ... CELLS!✳

All living things are made of cells. Our bodies are made of zillions and zillions of cells, for example.

These first cells were very simple, though. They were BACTERIA, and all they could do was soak up food and divide into more cells.

Before long, there were lots of different bacteria floating about. Most of them still soaked up their food from the water. But a few of them used something called CHLOROPHYLL to make their own food.

And one kind in particular, called BLUE-GREEN BACTERIA, had discovered how to do something really special.

These blue-greens didn't look like much — just clumps of scummy green stuff, floating around in the oceans.

Like some other cells, they used chlorophyll to make their own food. But the blue-greens also used something the other cells didn't. They used *water!*

And as there was lots of water around, there were soon lots of blue-greens about, too.

The *really special* thing the blue-greens did, though, was that as they made their food, they also gave off a waste gas.

And they went on giving it off for millions and millions of years — until the whole atmosphere was thick with it.

And guess what that waste gas was. It was OXYGEN — the very same stuff that we *breathe* today!

At this point there's another gap in the story, because nobody's really sure how the next part happened, either. But millions of years later, there were a whole lot of *new cells* on the scene.

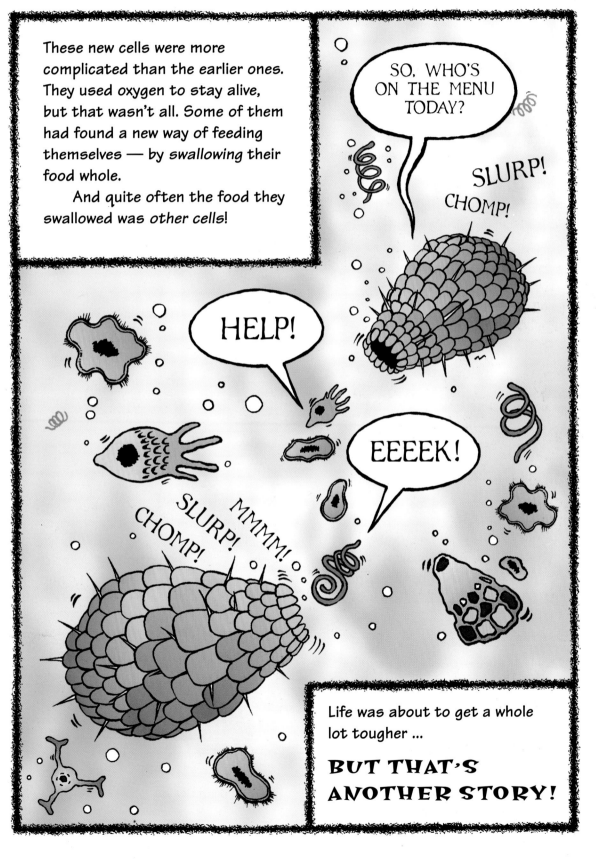

These new cells were more complicated than the earlier ones. They used oxygen to stay alive, but that wasn't all. Some of them had found a new way of feeding themselves — by *swallowing* their food whole.

And quite often the food they swallowed was *other cells*!

SO, WHO'S ON THE MENU TODAY?

SLURP!

CHOMP!

HELP!

EEEEK!

MMMM!

SLURP!

CHOMP!

Life was about to get a whole lot tougher ...

BUT THAT'S ANOTHER STORY!

A Cosmic Time Trail

13 billion years ago — The Big Bang happens.

5 billion years ago — The Sun starts to form.

It's not easy keeping track of time, especially when it's billions of years.✱ And since the events in this book took place long, long before anybody was around to record them, no one can be sure exactly when they happened.

4.6 billion years ago — The Earth and other planets start to form.

But by studying the stars and planets, and the different rocks on Earth, scientists have worked out some dates for when they think these events happened.

4–3.5 billion years ago — The Earth's crust hardens, the atmosphere and the oceans form, and life begins.

3.5–3 billion years ago — Bacteria flourish in the oceans, and blue-greens give out oxygen.

✱ A billion, by the way, is one thousand million or, if you like lots of zeros, it's 1 000 000 000.

1.2 billion years ago — Lots of new cells appear (today, scientists call these cells "protists").

Strange but True!

It's only in the last 200 years that we've discovered how old our planet truly is. Before this, people thought the Earth was just a few thousands of years old.

Back in 1650, an archbishop called James Ussher carefully added together the ages of all of the main characters in the Bible and figured out that the Earth was created in October, 4004 B.C. (that's about 6000 years ago).

John Lightfoot, a scholar at Cambridge University in England, then worked out that the time of creation must have been 9 A.M. *precisely*, on Sunday, 23 October, 4004 B.C.!

Facts about the Planets

☆ MERCURY

Average distance from Sun: 58 million km
   (36 million mi.)
Diameter across equator: 4878 km (3031 mi.)
Number of moons: 0
One complete spin: 59 Earth days
One orbit of the Sun: 88 Earth days
Size compared to Earth: x 0.38

☆ VENUS

Average distance from Sun: 108 million km
   (67 million mi.)
Diameter across equator: 12 104 km
   (7521 mi.)
Number of moons: 0
One complete spin: 243 Earth days
One orbit of the Sun:
   225 Earth days
Size compared to Earth: x 0.95

☆ EARTH

Average distance from Sun: 150 million km
   (93 million mi.)
         Diameter across equator: 12 756 km
            (7926 mi.)
         Number of moons: 1
         One complete spin: 23 hrs 56 mins
      One orbit of the Sun: 365.25 days
Size compared to Earth: x 1

☆ MARS

Average distance from Sun: 228 million km
   (142 million mi.)
Diameter across equator: 6787 km
   (4217 mi.)
Number of moons: 2
One complete spin: 24 Earth hrs 37 mins
One orbit of the Sun: 687 Earth days
Size compared to Earth: x 0.53

☆ JUPITER

Average distance from Sun: 778 million km
   (438 million mi.)
Diameter across equator: 142 984 km
   (88 700 mi.)
Number of moons: 16
One complete spin: 9 Earth hrs 55 mins
One orbit of the Sun: 11.9 Earth years
Size compared to Earth: x 11.20

☆ SATURN

Average distance from Sun:
   1427 million km
   (886 million mi.)
Diameter across equator: 120 536 km
   (74 600 mi.)
Number of moons: at least 18
One complete spin: 10 Earth hrs 40 mins
One orbit of the Sun: 29.5 Earth years
Size compared to Earth: x 9.45

☆ URANUS

Average distance from Sun:
   2871 million km
   (1723 million mi.)
Diameter across equator: 51 118 km
   (30 671 mi.)
Number of moons: at least 18
One complete spin: 17 Earth hrs 17 mins
One orbit of the Sun: 84 Earth years
Size compared to Earth: x 4

☆ NEPTUNE

Average distance from Sun:
   4497 million km
   (2698 million mi.)
Diameter across equator: 49 528 km
   (29 717 mi.)
Number of moons: 8
One complete spin: 16 Earth hrs 5 mins
One orbit of the Sun: 165 Earth years
Size compared to Earth: x 3.88

☆ PLUTO

Average distance from Sun: 5914 million km
   (3548 million mi.)
Diameter across equator: 2300 km
   (1380 mi.)
Number of moons: 1
One complete spin: 6 Earth days 9 hrs
One orbit of the Sun: 248.5 Earth years
Size compared to Earth: x 0.18

 = Earth in scale
to planets

Glossary

When you see a word here in CAPITAL LETTERS LIKE THIS, it means that this word has a separate entry of its own where you can find more information.

ASTEROID A rocky object that ORBITS the SUN and that measures anything from 2 to 700 km (1 to 420 mi.) in DIAMETER. Most asteroids orbit in a belt between Mars and Jupiter. Others wander around the SOLAR SYSTEM on orbits of their own, and some come quite close to Earth. One or two may even have collided with our planet in the past.

ATMOSPHERE A layer of GASES that surrounds some of the PLANETS in our SOLAR SYSTEM.

BACTERIA One of the simplest forms of life there is. There are thousands of different sorts of bacteria, and they can live almost anywhere. Most are so tiny they can only be seen through a microscope. Some are harmful, but others are vital to life on Earth.

BIG BANG An enormously powerful explosion that many people think was the beginning of our UNIVERSE.

BLUE-GREEN BACTERIA An early life-form that still exists today. They separate hydrogen from water and use it with CHLOROPHYLL, sunlight and carbon dioxide to make food. If you take HYDROGEN from water, you're left with OXYGEN. Blue-green bacteria give off oxygen as a waste gas.

CELL A cell is a single unit of life. Some simple life-forms are made of just one cell, but most living things are made of thousands or even billions of cells.

CHEMICALS The general name given to the materials that make up all the different kinds of gases, liquids and solids — such as HYDROGEN, OXYGEN, carbon and iron, for example.

CHLOROPHYLL A green CHEMICAL that soaks up energy from sunlight. Green plants (and a few other things) use this energy to make food from carbon dioxide and HYDROGEN.

COMET A lump of rock and ice a few kilometers (miles) across that ORBITS the SUN. Comets can have huge orbits. There are billions of them that we never see. They lie beyond the PLANETS, at the very edge of the SOLAR SYSTEM. But some comets have orbits that bring them close to the Sun. Then they heat up and give off a trail of GAS that glows in the Sun's light.

DIAMETER The distance across the center of a circle, or through the widest part of a round object, from one side to the other.

DUST When GASES from stars are flung into space, some of them cool down and join together to make tiny specks of dust.

GALAXY An enormous group of stars. Each galaxy in the UNIVERSE may contain thousands of millions of stars. Galaxies also contain GAS clouds from which new stars are born. Galaxies are held together by GRAVITY, and all the stars in a galaxy are slowly turning around the galaxy's center. Our galaxy, the Milky Way, has at least 200 000 million stars and takes about 220 million years to turn around once.

GAS One of three ways in which MATTER can exist — as a liquid, a solid or a gas. If a gas gets cold enough, or if it is squashed together tightly enough, it will turn into a liquid or even a solid. Most of the matter in the UNIVERSE is gas.

GRAVITY Gravity is a pulling force that tugs everything towards everything else. It is gravity that keeps the PLANETS going around the SUN and the MOONS traveling around the planets. And it is gravity that keeps our feet on the ground — without it, everything on Earth's surface would float off into space.

HELIUM AND HYDROGEN The two most common CHEMICALS in the UNIVERSE. They are usually GASES, but they can be liquids.

MATTER The stuff that makes up the UNIVERSE. Matter can exist as a solid, a liquid or a gas.

MOON A rocky object that ORBITS a PLANET. Like planets, moons do not give out any light of their own.

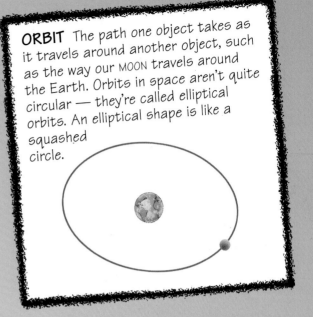

ORBIT The path one object takes as it travels around another object, such as the way our MOON travels around the Earth. Orbits in space aren't quite circular — they're called elliptical orbits. An elliptical shape is like a squashed circle.

OXYGEN The GAS that most living things on Earth need in order to survive. About one-fifth of the Earth's ATMOSPHERE is made up of oxygen.

PLANET A large object that ORBITS a star. Planets do not give out any light of their own. They can only be seen because they reflect the light of the star they are orbiting.

SOLAR SYSTEM The name given to the group of PLANETS and any other objects that ORBIT a star. Not all stars have solar systems.

SUN The name we give to our star. The Sun is at the center of our SOLAR SYSTEM. Like all stars, it is mostly made of HYDROGEN GAS. Its DIAMETER is more than 100 times bigger than the Earth's. At its center, the temperature of the Sun reaches an amazing 15 million° C (27 million° F).

SUPERNOVA The explosion that sometimes happens when a really large star dies. The gassy outer layers of the star are hurled into space and all that's left is a small, incredibly squashed lump of MATTER.

UNIVERSE The Universe is everything — the whole of space and everything in it.

Index

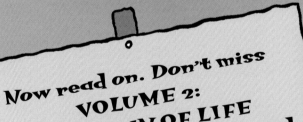

Now read on. Don't miss VOLUME 2: THE DAWN OF LIFE How cells got together and life took to the land!